WHY DOES

the Moon change shape?

By Helen Orme

helping to explain the solar system

WHY DOES

the Moon change shape?

Copyright © ticktock Entertainment Ltd 2003
First published in Great Britain in 2003 by ticktock Media Ltd.,
Unit 2, Orchard Business Centre, North Farm Road, Tunbridge Wells, Kent, TN2 3XF
We would like to thank: Lorna Cowan, Robert Massey of the Royal Observatory
and Elizabeth Wiggans.
ISBN 1 86007 387 5 pbk
ISBN 1 86007 393 X hbk
Printed in China
A CIP catalogue record for this book is available from the British Library.

CONTENTS

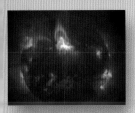

Any words appearing in the text in bold,
like this, are explained in the Glossary.

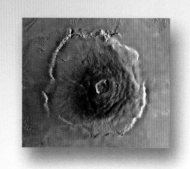

What can you see
when you look at
the night sky?

Moon

Planets

Solar System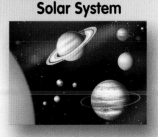

You might see a big shining object called the Moon. You might see lots of little bright lights called **stars**. You can even see some larger, bright objects called **planets**. The Moon, the planets and one star you know called the Sun make up the **Solar System.**

All the planets go round (**orbit**) the Sun.

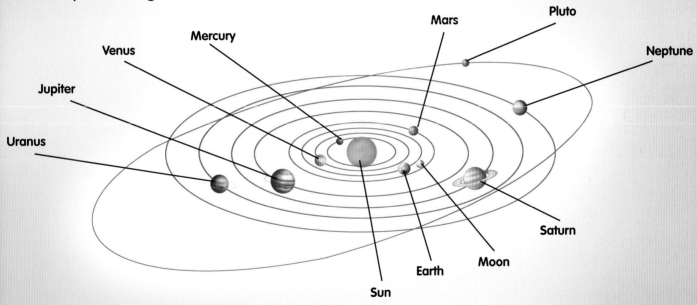

How many planets are there in the Solar System?

What do the planets look like?

Which planet in the Solar System do you live on?

Why is the Sun so important?

The Sun is a small **star**.

A star makes heat and light by turning **hydrogen gas** into **helium gas**.

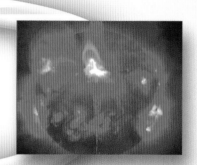

Without the Sun our **planet** would always be dark and freezing cold. We would not be able to live here.

The sun gives the warmth that makes living things grow.

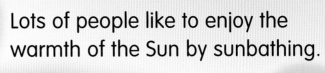

Lots of people like to enjoy the warmth of the Sun by sunbathing.

The Sun is a long way from us, but its heat is so powerful it can burn you if you stay out too long.

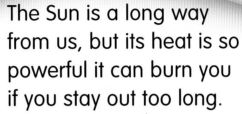

How long would it take to walk to the Sun?

(answer on p23)

Remember

You must never look directly at the Sun. It can blind you.

The Sun is the centre of the **Solar System**. All the other planets travel round (or **orbit**) it.

Which do you think are the nearest planets to the Sun?

a) Mercury and Venus

b) Mars

c) Earth

(You will find the answer on the next page.)

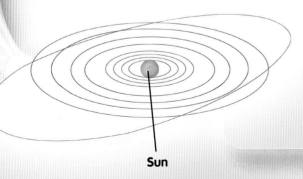

Sun

Which planets are nearest to the Sun?

Mercury

Venus

Mercury is the nearest **planet** to the Sun.

Do you think you could live on Mercury?

(answer on p23)

Mercury is the smallest of all the planets.

Mercury

Venus

It is so hot on Mercury that metal would **melt** on its **surface**.

Venus is the second planet from the Sun. It is very, very hot.

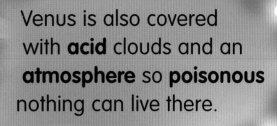

Venus is also covered with **acid** clouds and an **atmosphere** so **poisonous** nothing can live there.

It is the closest planet to us.

By using a **telescope** you can see Venus in even more detail.

If you look in the morning, you can see Venus rising before the Sun comes up.

Which planet is a good place to live?

a) Mars

b) Earth

c) Jupiter

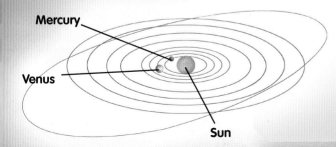

Mercury

Venus

Sun

9

Which planet is a good place to live?

The Earth is a good place to live. It is neither too hot nor too cold. Earth is our home.

It is the only **planet** that we know of where people, animals and plants can live.

A lot of the **surface** is covered with water. All living things need water to drink.

Earth's air also has enough **oxygen** to let us breathe.

Some places on Earth are very hot, like this rainforest.

Some are very cold, like the Antarctic (the South Pole).

Why is the Earth such a good place to live?

(answer on 23)

The Earth is just right for all types of life. From the very tiny...

...to the very large!

Mercury

s

Sun   Earth

Why does the moon change shape?

a) Because different amounts of it are in shadow

b) Because it melts from the Sun's heat

c) Because it is shrinking

Why does the Moon change shape?

The Moon is always circling Earth.

It takes just one month for the Moon to make one round trip.

Half of the Moon is lit by the Sun and half is in **shadow**. Different amounts of the Moon's face are lit up depending on where the Moon is. This is why the Moon appears to change shape.

We know a lot about the moon because it has been visited by **space probes** and by **astronauts** in **spacecraft**.

What spacecraft do modern astronauts fly to the Moon in?

(answer on p23)

The Moon has no water, no weather and no air.

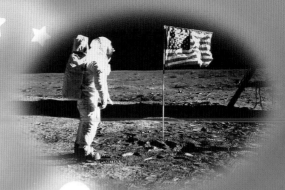

When astronauts visited the Moon they had to wear special **spacesuits** to help them breathe.

The **surface** of the Moon is covered with holes called **craters**. They are made when lumps of rock from space hit the Moon.

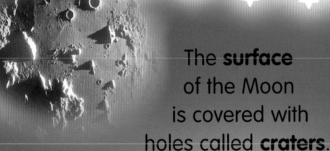

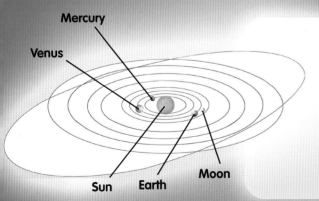

Mercury

Venus

Sun   Earth   Moon

Why is Mars called the Red Planet?

a) Because of the colour of the soil

b) Because of the aliens living there

c) Because it is very hot

Why is Mars called the Red Planet?

When you see Mars through a **telescope** it looks quite red.

This is not because it is hot, but because it has very red soil.

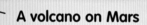
A volcano on Mars

Mars is smaller than Earth. But it has two moons, and the biggest **volcano** in the **Solar System**.

No **astronaut** has ever gone to Mars, but **spacecraft** have visited the planet.

It takes spacecraft about six months to reach Mars.

Scientists know there is frozen water on Mars.

They also think they have found **fossil bacteria** on rocks from Mars. This makes some people think there was once life there.

Do you think we could live on Mars?

(answer on p23)

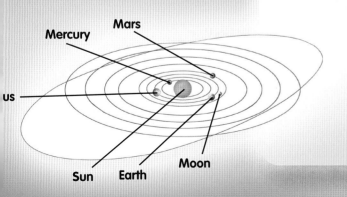

Mercury

Mars

us

Sun   Earth   Moon

Which are the biggest planets in the Solar System?

a) Jupiter and Saturn

b) Mercury and Venus

c) Neptune and Uranus

Which planets are the biggest?

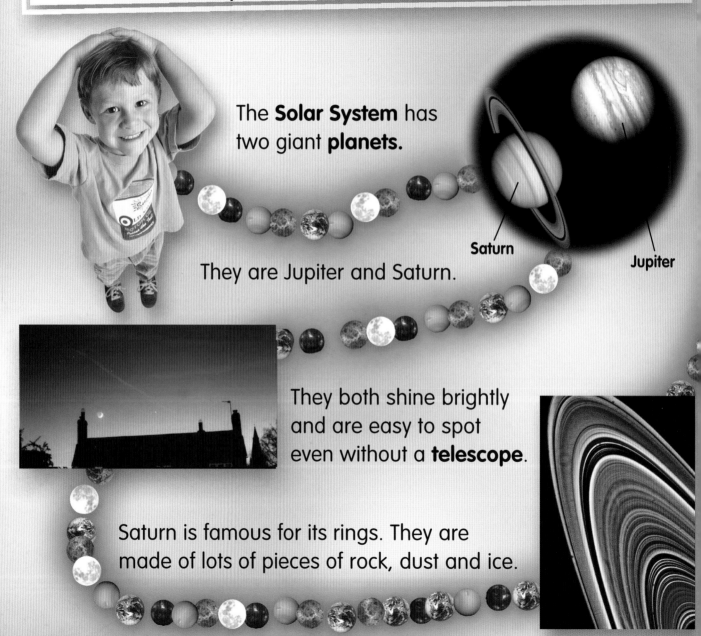

The **Solar System** has two giant **planets.**

They are Jupiter and Saturn.

Saturn

Jupiter

They both shine brightly and are easy to spot even without a **telescope**.

Saturn is famous for its rings. They are made of lots of pieces of rock, dust and ice.

Jupiter is the biggest planet in the Solar System.

It is twice as large as all the other planets put together.

Through a powerful telescope you can see that Jupiter is surrounded by bands of **gas**.

How many rings does Saturn have?

(answer on p23)

Red spot

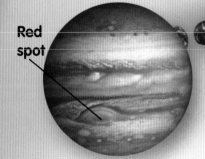

Jupiter also has a giant red spot. This is actually a massive storm that has been blowing for years.

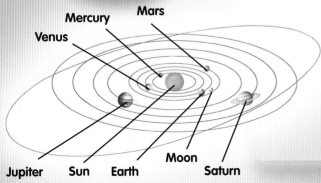

Mercury
Mars
Venus
Jupiter Sun Earth Moon Saturn

Which planets are farthest away from us?

a) Neptune and Pluto
b) Mercury and Venus
c) Jupiter and Saturn

Which planets are farthest away from us?

Uranus

Neptune

Pluto

Uranus, Neptune and Pluto
are far, far away from the Sun.

Pluto

Neptune

Uranus

Because they are so
far away from the Sun,
its light is too weak
to warm them up much.

They are cold, icy
planets, colder than the
coldest place on Earth.

What do you
think would
happen if you
landed on Pluto?

(answer on p23)

Space probes have flown past Neptune and Uranus to find out more about the planets.

These planets are very stormy places. A storm spot just like the one on Jupiter has been seen on Neptune.

Neptune's storm spot

Pluto is the farthest planet from the Sun. It is so far away we don't know much about it.

A space probe called New Horizons will visit Pluto in 2015 to find out more.

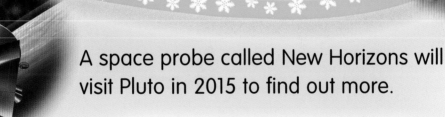

Pluto

Neptune

Mars

Mercury

Venus

Uranus

Jupiter

Sun   Earth

Moon

Saturn

What is Deep Space?

a) A place under the sea

b) The area outside the Solar System

c) A really heavy part of space

What is Deep Space?

Deep Space includes everything in the **Universe** beyond Earth.

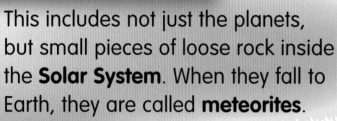

This includes not just the planets, but small pieces of loose rock inside the **Solar System**. When they fall to Earth, they are called **meteorites**.

Sometimes much bigger rocks called **asteroids** crash into Earth. This huge **crater** was made by an asteroid.

But Deep Space doesn't end there. Our **Solar System** is just a tiny part of a **galaxy** called the Milky Way. There are many other galaxies too.

Scientists use special equipment to investigate beyond the Solar System.

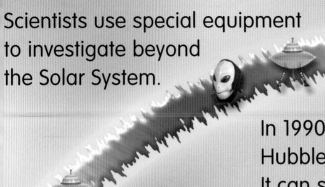

In 1990 **NASA** launched the Hubble Space **Telescope**. It can see far out into space.

Scientists even send **space probes** to photograph **stars** we cannot see from Earth.

How many people have flown in space?

(answer on p23)

THE SOUNDS OF EARTH

UNITED STATES OF AMERICA
PLANET EARTH

In case they make contact with other **lifeforms**, some space probes carry discs telling listeners things about our planet.

21

Glossary

Acid A chemical substance that can burn or eat away organic tissues, such as skin, and many other materials.

Asteroids Large rocks in space the size of small planets.

Astronauts People who travel in space.

Atmosphere The air that surrounds a planet.

Craters Holes in a surface made by rocks hitting it, or by volcanoes.

Deep Space The area of the Universe beyond Earth.

Fossil bacteria The remains of tiny organisms (living things) that lived in an earlier time and became embedded in rock.

Galaxy A huge grouping of stars.

Gas When some things are heated they turn into a gas. Water turns into a gas called steam. The air we breathe is made from many gases.

Helium gas A colourless gas with no smell. The Sun makes its energy by changing hydrogen into helium.

Hydrogen gas A light gas that burns easily. The Sun turns hydrogen into helium to make energy.

Life forms Living things.

Melt When a solid turns into a liquid, usually because it has been heated.

Meteorites Chunks of rock that have broken off from an asteroid and fallen to Earth.

NASA (National Aeronautics and Space Administration) An organisation in the USA. They send spacecraft into space to study our solar system and beyond.

Orbit To move round something in a set path.

Oxygen A part of the air

needed by people and
animals to breathe.

Planet A ball of rock or gas that
goes round (orbits) the Sun.

Poisonous Dangerous
to eat, drink or breathe.

Shadow Dark area created
by the blocking of light.

Solar System A name for
the Sun and the planets
and moons that go round it.

Spacecraft A ship made
to travel in space.

Spacesuits Clothes astronauts
wear to protect them in space.

Space probes Spacecraft
without people on them

that explore space.

Stars Large balls of burning
gas, far away in space.

Surface The outside part of
a planet or moon, or the top
part of something, like the sea.

Telescope Something we look
through. It makes things seem
closer and more detailed.

Volcano A place where hot,
melted rocks come up to
the surface from deep in
the ground.

Universe Everything
in space, including the Earth,
Solar System and galaxies.

Could you answer all the questions? Here are the answers:

Page 7: It would take nearly 3,000 years for a person to walk to the Sun!

Page 8: Not a good idea. Mercury's atmosphere is so poisonous nothing can live there.

Page 11: The Earth has air we can breathe, water we can drink and it is the perfect temperature for life.

Page 13: Astronauts today use the Space Shuttle for missions to the Moon.

Page 15: Not at the moment, but some scientists think that we might be able to build a base on Mars in the future.

Page 17: When the Voyager spacecraft flew past Saturn, it counted thousands of rings.

Page 18: It is so cold on Pluto that your body would freeze solid in under a minute.

Page 21: 1,720 people have been sent into space so far.

Index

**t=top, b=bottom, c=centre, l=left, r=right,
OFC=outside front cover, OBC=outside back cover**

**Alamy: 4br & OFC, 7tr, 7cl, 8bl, 9br, 12cl, 15r, 16tl, 17cr.
Creatas: 19cr. NASA: 2tl, 2bl, 3tl, 3tr, 3bl, 3br, 4cl, 4cr, 4bl and OBC, 5tl,
6cr, 8tl, 12tl, 12br, 13tl, 13cl, 13cr, 14tl, 14tr, 14cl, 14b, 15tl, 16tr, 16br, 17tl,
17cl, 18tl, 18cr, 19tl, 19tc, 19bl & OBC, 20cr, 21tr, 21c, 21b, 22tl, 22tr, 22b,
22bc, 22br, 23tr, 23bl, 23br, 24bl, 24tr.**